# GREEN SUSTAINABLE ECONOMICS

(AN EVERGREEN PHASE OF DIVINE LAW)

# BY: DEBT JUBILEE PUBLISHERS

(PRINTED ON Q4 2021)

# TABLE OF CONTENTS

1. CITIZENSHIP OF THE KINGDOM OF GOD: 3-13
2. ECONOMIC FREEDOM AND SECURITY: 14-23
3. THE PROBLEM OF DISTRIBUTION: 24-34
4. A STABLE VALUE OF MONEY: 35-42
5. JESUS, ECONOMIST: 43-52

# 1. CITIZENSHIP OF THE KINGDOM OF GOD

In this modern world the Bible occupies a less important place in the thoughts of men than in the days of our ancestors. Some ascribe this to the outmoding of superstition by the so-called superior knowledge and wisdom of an enlightened <u>scientific age</u> (1 Timothy 6:20). Others, while receiving the spiritual message of the Bible, fail to see in it the solution of our economic and social problems.

Yet both Old and New Testaments contain a revelation of God's Will, eternal principles which are the only true guide for mankind from age to age. In spite of the drift away from the Bible, the need is greater than ever before to learn Divine Wisdom and obey the Divine Will.

The closer the enquiry into the works of the Creator, the more obvious it becomes that there is a right and a wrong way of doing things. Throughout all is the reign of law. <u>Obedience</u> to The Law tends to Life, <u>disobedience</u> tends to Death. Obedience to the laws of electricity has supplied many wonderful inventions for the comfort and convenience of mankind. Disobedience of the law of insulation is death.

The law of fertility of the soil has been termed the Wheel of Life. Death and decay are transmuted into life and health by the harmonious (organic) action of bacteria, fungi and worms in the soil. The true basis of public health should be the law of return of animal and vegetable wastes to the soil, yet in our time the <u>chemical mind</u> has neglected this Wisdom. Analysis of soil chemicals has posed as scientific knowledge, and dosing the land with this or that chemical compound has been the vain remedy for sickness of the soil. The unexpected result of that way is soil erosion, dustbowls, deserts, polluted drinking-water, more diseases, sickness and death.

In modern times the doctrines of finance capitalism have held the stage. The so-called science of economics has been enthroned. The miseries of the workers in the 18th and 19th centuries, the dire poverty of the masses in contrast with the fabulous riches of the few, these were regarded as regrettable evils, but inevitable, as part of the man-made "laws of economics". Men have failed to realise that the system of finance capitalism was made by man, and had no part in the Wisdom of God. The evils are inevitable only as long as the evil system which causes them is allowed to endure and prevail.

So we turn to <u>the Bible</u> for the solution of the problem. We find that economics has an important place in God's Will, but we also find that economics cannot be separated from the larger questions of right relationship between God and man, and between man and man. We find the chief Law to be, Mark 12:30-31: "Thou shalt love the Lord thy God with all thy heart, and with all thy soul, and with all thy mind and with all thy strength and Him only shalt thou serve. And the second is like it, Thou shalt love thy neighbour as thyself."

In the beginning God created man and woman, whose happiness and welfare depends upon obedience to His Commands. Worldly counsels, however, prevailed; the lust of the <u>flesh</u>, the desire of the eyes, and the pride of life were preferred to the Wisdom of God. The result was death. In the same hour that the sentence of death was passed, came the promise. The seed of the woman should bruise the head of the serpent, but the serpent would bruise his heel. The long genealogies that follow in the Bible were recorded in the hope of the coming of the seed of the Woman, the expected Redeemer of mankind. The hopes of The Covenant seed were in the future. When Jesus came in fulfillment of the promise, the powers of evil sought to destroy Him, but He rose from the grave triumphant over sin and death.

The Bible teaches believers in Jesus to look forward to <u>His return in power</u>, when they hope to be changed into His likeness, and they expect that the "dead" in Christ shall also be raised in the new body of eternal life. This is the Gospel of Salvation, and is expressed in the words of Jesus, John 3:16, "For God so loved the world that He gave His only begotten Son, that whosoever believeth Him should not perish, but have everlasting life."

The Bible contains another theme which is termed the Gospel of the Kingdom of God. <u>Abraham</u> was called to inherit a certain land, to found a great nation, and to be a blessing to all families of the Earth. In due time his descendants, the twelve tribes of Israel, entered into Palestine with the promise that, if they obeyed God's voice, they would be unto Him a kingdom of priests, and an holy nation. They were being established as God's Model Kingdom on Earth, to obey His Law, and to be prosperous and happy. Other nations would observe this shining example of how God's Law works in human affairs, and wish to do likewise.

Israel, as Bible history shows, rarely obeyed God's Laws. They became a melancholy example of the frustrations which follow departure from The Right Way of doing things. The two Israel nations (for early in their career they divided into two kingdoms, the northern ten-tribed House of Israel, and the southern two-tribed House of Judah; Judah [Jew-dah] being the ancestor of some of the Jews) went successively into captivity and exile.

Some of the Jews returned from exile, and it was to them Jesus came preaching the Gospel of the Kingdom of God. He gave them another chance to obey God's Law and to become God's Model Kingdom on Earth; but they rejected Him, and therefore He declared that the Kingdom of God was taken from them and would be given to a nation bringing forth the fruits of it.

The attempt of the Zionists to claim Palestine as the national home of the Jews is unscriptural on several grounds, and its fruit is the insoluble Palestine problem, and may well be the Sarajevo to kindle into flame the Third World War. It ignores the fact that the Jews are descended from only two of the twelve tribes of Israel. It ignores the fact that no promise of national restoration is made in the Scriptures apart from the New Covenant in Christ. It forgets that the wider promise to Jacob was that his seed should spread abroad to the West, and to the East, and to the North and to the South, and that the blessings would be to the "utmost bounds of the everlasting hills."

We, of the British Commonwealth of nations (Ephraim - Genesis 48:19) have, through no conscious effort of our own, come to occupy a unique position in the world, with a unique opportunity to put God's Law into practice, and be a blessing to other nations. This position and opportunity are shared by the United States of America (Manasseh - Genesis 48:19). Instead, we have enthroned the false gods of finance capitalism, and unless we set our own house in order, the opportunity will pass us by also. It is therefore an urgent matter for us to become acquainted with God's Law, that we may find the solution of the problems which so grievously perplex our age.

When both houses of Israel were going into captivity, the prophets received God's promise that He would write His Law in the hearts of His people Israel, Jesus supplied the key to this promise when He said "If ye love Me, keep My Commandments." And again, John 3:3, "Except a man be born again (as his spirit-Being, which is not human), he cannot see the Kingdom of God."

Obedience to God's Law is the result of the new birth (as your spirit-Being). The sinful <u>nature</u> of the flesh (human) can not do God's Will, only the new spiritual life with the Spirit of God through faith in Christ Jesus can keep The Law. Thus the Gospel of Salvation and the Gospel of the Kingdom become <u>one organic whole</u>.

In the Kingdom of God, Christ will be King. Every great war has been followed by a <u>League of Nations or a U.N.O.</u>, but every such attempt to bring concord and security to mankind has ended in disaster, because it has been built on faulty foundations (Ezekiel 13:9-16). The citizens of the Kingdom of God must be born again as their spirit-Being, and they must <u>acknowledge Christ as Lord and King</u>.

## 2. ECONOMIC FREEDOM AND SECURITY

In modern times very few are economically free. Most are dependent on others for their employment and for the means of subsistence. The employers are frequently in their turn dependent on the will of those who hold the power of capitalist finance. If any be fortunate enough to possess land it is unusually encumbered by mortgage, and freedom is brought into the bondage of debt.

The Bible Laws of Economics assure freedom and independence to EVERY family. When Israel obtained the promised land, it was divided as fairly as possible so that EVERY family should receive its portion. The land was free from debt and the only tax was a tenth part of the fruit of the soil, the tithe being the inheritance of the Levites, who, being engaged in work of national importance, had no land.

The land was inherited, free of death duties, from generation to generation. It had no money value, and must not be sold for ever. The possessors of the land were regarded, not as the owners (for the land was God's, Leviticus 25:23), but as <u>God's guests</u>.

Should circumstances compel, it was permitted to sell the land, but the price should be adjusted according to the number of years to the Jubilee. The price was not for the land itself, but for its produce. In the fiftieth, the Year of Jubilee, every family must return to its inheritance. This great event must take place on the 10th day of the 7th month, the Day of Atonement, on which all the people made confession of their sins; it was a day for national repentance. Thus were closely related the economic and religious life of the nation. It was not a day of bondage, but a day of freedom, a day of new beginnings.

"And ye shall hallow the fiftieth year, and proclaim liberty throughout all the land unto all the inhabitants thereof: it shall be a jubilee unto you; and ye shall return every man unto his possession, and ye shall return every man unto his family." (Leviticus 25:10).

The <u>United States of America</u> claim to be the land of the free, and a portion of the above quotation was inscribed on their Liberty Bell: "Proclaim liberty throughout the land unto all the inhabitants thereof." But the rest of The Law was omitted, and that is why the United States of America are just as much subject to financial and industrial troubles as any other nation which departs from God's Law.

The Law of Inheritance was at one time deeply written in the conscience of ancient Israel. When the despotic king Ahab coveted Naboth's vineyard, even he was unable to obtain possession against Naboth's will. It was only when his consort Jezebel had suborned the elders of the people to accept false witness and pronounce judgment of death for treason, that the king was able to seize the land.

Others exercised their unscrupulous skill in accumulating land, for we find Isaiah (5:8) declaring "Woe unto them that join house to house, that lay field to field, that they may be placed alone in the midst of the earth!"

The Jews who returned from Babylon met with drought, and some were hard put to it to find food for themselves, much less the corn and money tribute to Babylon. These were compelled to mortgage their lands and houses to their wealthier compatriots. When Nehemiah, the new Governor, saw the state of affairs he set up a Mortgage Corporation, fixed the rate of interest at 5 per cent, and caused placards to be posted up in public places promising security to the investors. No, I have that wrong. I am quoting from a proclamation of the <u>New Zealand</u> Government in the early nineteen thirties. Nehemiah said: "I was very angry when I heard their cry and these words. Then I consulted with myself, and rebuked the nobles, and the rulers, and said unto them, Ye exact usury, every one of his brother. And I set a great assembly against them. . . Then held they their peace, and had nothing to answer. . . Restore, I pray you, to them, even this day, their lands, their vineyards, and their houses, also the hundredth part of the money and the corn, and the wine, and the oil, that ye exact of them. Then said they, We will restore them, and will require nothing of them; so will we do as thou sayest."

A rich young man came to Jesus claiming that he had kept The Laws of Moses from his youth up; but Jesus put His finger on the vital spot. How did this man's family accumulate such great possessions? Let him sell all, and give to the poor.

Thus in Israel, while every family was assured of a sufficient living, no man could lawfully accumulate large holdings at the expense of others.

The clans of Scotland followed the patriarchal system of the Old Testament/Covenant. Every crofter had his holding. The yeomen of England were likewise free and independent by virtue of their land. The industrial revolution and the enclosure of land changed all this, creating a great landless labouring class at the mercy of others for their precarious and ill-paid jobs.

Since then, conditions of labour and rates of pay have been improved by legislation, but modern economics are now dominated by the machine and mass production. Money and the machine, which should be our beneficent servants, have become our ruthless masters.

Many say that the old Laws of Israel, with their rural patriarchal conditions, are out of date. Others, with truer visions, see in them our salvation. The prophet of old foresaw that in the new age every man would dwell under his own vine and fig tree. Is it possible to do away with machines, put every man back on the land, and return to peasant life? Perhaps not, but it IS possible to decentralise industry, giving each worker sufficient land to occupy his increasing leisure. It IS possible to place more and more on small holdings with profit to themselves and to the community. It IS possible to foster a renewed love of and respect for the land, to breed a race of husbandmen.

God warned of this going away from His Divine Laws, Economics and the land and the ensuing envy, competition, strife, chaos and wars it would create and gave the solution to these ills when He said: "Beat your swords into plough-shares and your spears into pruning-hooks and learn war (competition) no more." (Isaiah 2:4 & Micah 4:3-5). In other words return to the Divine Laws, Economics and the land of (with) plenty.

In Tahiti, at the age of sixteen, a young man is allotted a plot of land, and he is free to marry. The land is his until he dies, when it reverts to the Crown. True, the Tahitians are a simple community, but they are free, and they have no national debt.

If we are to retain the (questionable) blessings of machine power (and the <u>pollution</u> created by them), the system of finance capitalism with debt and interest must be abolished. In building a new system we must bear in mind the foundation principle of God's Law — that every person is entitled to a share in the fruits of the soil. It is not possible for every man to possess land and to work entirely on it, but every secondary industry also depends upon the land for its raw materials and the workers for their food from it. Every worker contributes to the wealth of the nation. Those who do not actually produce add their services to the common pool.

The sum total of national constructive effort is the true basis of the issue of money, whether in the form of currency or of credit. If the total productive power of the nation can be computed and the national income distributed in fair proportion to every person, irrespective of the nature of the employment, the result would be the same as giving everybody a share in the land itself.

Thus would the first principle of Divine Economic Law be obeyed — economic freedom and security for ALL. (No deprivation and therefore no reason to <u>steal or commit crime</u> in order to survive). It is not God's Law that is out of step with mankind, but mankind that is drastically and criminally out of step with God and His Laws (James 4).

## 3. THE PROBLEM OF DISTRIBUTION

In Study 2 we have seen that God's Law provides economic freedom and security for all. In Israel, the land itself was divided among all the people, each family with its inheritance. Those who can grow their own food, build their own houses, and make their own clothing have economic freedom, which is more real than mere political freedom.

For those who practise self-sufficient husbandry, the problem of distribution of food is of the simplest. It is consumed where it is grown (no lorries polluting the atmosphere to deliver food to the cities; no packaging to have to recycle, landfill or incinerate). Any dependents of the family, aged, young, or cripple, would receive their share from the common store. Surplus might be traded in the nearest town for clothing or other manufactures. Trade might extend far and wide, as indeed it did in the days of Solomon.

In such a community could there be poverty? There might be drought, fire, or even sloth and drunkenness. There might be many ways to poverty, none of which was specified in the Books of The Law. Poverty there was, because Laws were framed for its relief. These Laws may be briefly summarised as the Law of Gleaning, the Law of Lending free of interest, and the Law of Forgiveness of Debts.

The corn must not be too closely harvested from the field, the grapes must not be too well garnered, the olive trees must not be shaken. The poor must be permitted to come and glean the generous remainder.

If any person required a loan of either money or goods, the loan must be free of interest.

"Usury" is the word, and some in our day regard usury only as excessive interest; but the meaning of the Bible is clear, for it is called "usury or increase." Any rate of increase would be usury (and be the cause of inflation). Israelites were (and still are) sadly apt to disobey this Law, but the sinfulness of usury was admitted. It was not respectable as (is wrongly believed) in our time. Ezekiel (22:6-12) classes taking usury and increase with carrying tales to shed blood, adultery, and incest. The 15th Psalm draws a portrait of a gentleman. "He that putteth not out his money to usury."

The seventh year was called the Year of Release. Read about it in the 15th chapter of Deuteronomy. Not only were all slaves released from bondage, but in that year all debts must be forgiven. "If there be among you a poor man . . . thou shalt not harden thine heart, nor shut thine hand from thy poor brother: but thou shalt open thine hand wide unto him sufficient for his need, in that which he wanteth. Beware that there be not a thought in thy wicked heart, saying, The seventh year, the year of release is at hand... Thou shalt surely give him, and thine heart shall not be grieved when thou givest unto him: because that for this thing the Lord thy God shall bless thee in all thy works, and in all that thou puttest thine hand unto."

Plenty to say about the duty of the lender. Not a word about how the poverty arose — bad fortune, laziness or sin — the cause of the poverty is not mentioned. The great fact is that here is a case of need, and here are the means of satisfying that need, and no question of loss must be considered. Out of the surplus of one is made up the lack of the other. We are not exalting laziness or sin. "The wicked borroweth, and payeth not again: but the righteous sheweth mercy, and giveth." (Psalm 37:21). The point is that the purpose of The Law is to satisfy the needs of every creature. Economic independence for all: but should that for some reason be lost, free sharing by those who are able.

This forgiveness of debts was taken by Jesus as an illustration of God's forgiveness of our sins. "Forgive us our debts as we forgive our debtors." A worldly Church has altered those words. "Forgive us our trespasses as we forgive them that trespass against us." (Matt. 6:12). Forgive an insult or injury? Yes, that is possible. But forgive a debt? Why, that would destroy the sanctity of contract! Yet so important in God's creative plan is the forgiveness of sins that His Son took the form of sinful flesh to pay the price for us. Sacrificial love is in it. And in the Divine

System of Economics is the same element of sacrificial love: free sharing and forgiveness of debts.

But many, even among Christians, argue that The Laws of lending free of interest and forgiveness of debts applied only in the case of poverty. They do not apply, they say, to modern industrial transactions. These people forget that modern times differ from the days of Israel in the lack of economic security. The Law provided an initial security for all, and only those who had fallen away need borrow. With us, most are in need. Every man building a house, starting a business, or taking up land is a man in need. He needs a loan.

Conditions of industrialism and mass production have reduced most people to poverty. Very few individuals are in the position to lend large sums. Most lending is done by banks, insurance companies, State Advances, or <u>churches</u>. These institutions have departed from the principles as well as the letter of God's Law. A pledge is always taken for debt, interest is always charged, and debts are never forgiven. God's answer to the problem of distribution is giving, free lending, and forgiveness of debts. By these methods the goods would be distributed quickly to all in need. The methods of finance capitalism limit loans to the creditworthy and ignore human need. Distribution of production is frustrated and impeded. The wheels of production are retarded, and in times of depression come to a standstill.

Often production is limited purposely to create a false shortage in order to artificially drive up the price of food and goods, so that the producer can obtain more money for less goods and work involved in production, thereby causing poverty and deprivation for others who do not have their own land and means of production.

The social credit analysis of modern industrial production reveals a gap between the volume of production and purchasing power distributed as wages and dividends. During the war, it is true, purchasing power exceeds the supply of available goods, for the people who stayed at home were paid for producing, not consumable goods, but munitions which those who went away were paid for distributing free to the enemy. But with peace, if the productive powers of the nation are not hampered by finance, by Government or by strikes, it should not be long before there is such a volume of consumer goods as once more to exceed the purchasing power. This would mean that goods would then be cheap and plentiful with prosperity for all.

Then, to obey the principles of God's Law, the surplus should be *given* to those who are in need. Let us begin with the aged, the invalids, the children and the mothers (the orphan and the widow). Let the Government issue credit and give it, sufficient for the need. As the tide of production rises, let the Government issue credit, as a national dividend, to all the people, sufficient to distribute the increasing surplus.

The Divine Laws of distribution depend upon <u>individual love</u>. As Jesus said, the chief Law is to love God, "and the second is like unto it. Thou shalt love thy neighbour as (much as or more than) thyself. On these two Laws hang all The Law and the Prophets (and what they prophesied would happen)." That is why the

Kingdom of God can be attained only by its citizens being <u>born again</u>. Selfishness and greed have no place in a Christian society.

But in those days the means of production were in the hands of individuals with the power to disburse the products. Now, that power is limited to sharing a few vegetables with neighbours. The means of production belong more and more to the community. Manufactures are financed by companies. Even farmers are little more than cogs in the wheel. Their production depends also upon makers of farm machinery and clothing. The interlocking of effort is so complete that in effect we are all units in the scheme of production by the community.

The result of this is to remove the responsibility of distributive justice from the individual to the community. The individual conscience becomes the community conscience. The aged and the sick are less a family responsibility and more a social responsibility. A community of loving individuals would see that pensions are adequate. Indeed, we all have the will to increase pensions, and they would be increased had the Government the power to apply the Divine Law and issue credit according to need. The hindrance is the debt and interest system of finance which restricts the power of creating credit to the trading banks. Let Government take the sovereign power of issuing currency and credit (rather than privately-owned Central Banks like the Bank of England and Federal Reserve Bank of the U.S.A.), and then it would be able to carry out the wishes of a benevolent people.

## 4. A STABLE VALUE OF MONEY

In ancient times money took the form of unminted silver or gold. The talent and the shekel were units of weight. Gold and silver were weighed out. When Abraham bought a field from Ephron, he "weighed to Ephron the silver, which he had named in the audience of the sons of Heth, four hundred shekels of silver, current money with the merchant."

In measuring corn or oil, standard measures were used, the ephah and the hin. A dishonest merchant could have two weights; a small shekel if he were paying out silver, and a heavier shekel if he were receiving silver. He might have two measures; a large ephah if he were buying corn, or a smaller ephah if he were selling. In this way the value of money could be manipulated by the possessor of an evil heart. These things apparently were done, for in Deuteronomy 25:13-16, the practice is sternly forbidden.

"Thou shalt not have in thy bag diverse weights, a great and a small. Thou shalt not have in thy house diverse measures, a great and a small. But thou shalt have a perfect and just weight, a perfect and just measure shalt thou have: that thy days may be lengthened in the land which the Lord thy God giveth thee. For all that do such things, and all that do unrighteously, are an abomination unto the Lord thy God."

Those who commit evil will become sick and die, if, on becoming sick, they do not recognise the reason for that sickness and desist from doing evil and repent - (John 5:14).

Well, that is one thing about which we are very particular. We have inspectors of weights and measures and it is a serious offence to give short measure. But stay! The talent and the shekel were used to weigh money. Do our inspectors concern themselves with the value of money? Have they the power to take action if the £ of to-day (1947) buys only 10/- (50p) worth of goods as compared with the £ before the war? They have no control over the value of money. That is for financiers, <u>and they are a law unto themselves</u>. Power and large profits accrue to those who know how to manipulate the value of money, and with liberal donations to party funds, there might be a knighthood or even a peerage in it. A grocer who is discovered with a false balance may go to gaol (prison), but the financier who raises or lowers the value of the £ wins honour and applause. But, mark you, "they that do such things are an abomination to the Lord thy God."

When the issue of currency and credit is limited by the amount of gold reserve in the bank, there is no true relationship between the volume of money and the volume of goods. There might be an abundant harvest, but unless the amount of money available is increased, the price of wheat or apples, or whatever it may be will fall. The relationship between the ephah (or lb./pound) and the shekel (£/pound) has been upset, just as surely as if it had been deliberately and dishonestly done (which of course it has and is being by the financiers and the "Hidden Hand" of the Synagogue of Satan, that Jesus warned everyone about in the Apocalypse-Revelation 2:9 & 3:9).

The method of orthodox finance in dealing with a too bountiful harvest in order to maintain prices is to destroy the abundance by dumping apples in the sea, or burning wheat in (steam powered - 1947) locomotives, (whilst the poor go hungry). The obvious and sensible remedy is to issue more currency or credit to equate with the increased amount of the harvest. Applied as a national dividend, the bounty of the apple crop or the wheat harvest would be immediately distributed to an appreciative people. It should be the business of a board of experts appointed by Government to keep a close watch on the volume of production and the available purchasing power, and to advise upon the issue or curtailment of new (interest-free) credit.

So far in this and previous studies reference has been made to the issue of credit only for consumption; age pensions, family allowances, national dividends. It is fitting now to describe a simple method of issuing credit for production, an automatic measure of value. Each stage of production would be financed by a credit from the (publicly-owned) Reserve Bank, such credit to be cancelled when the loan is repaid or forgiven. The farmer would require long-term credits, but manufacturer, wholesaler, and retailer could use short-term commercial bills, which may be discounted for a very small rate to cover clerical expenses. As each transaction is completed, the bill is redeemed and the credit cancelled. The advance has been exactly according to the production, the commercial bill having acted as the measure of value.

The retailer is in rather a different position. If the wages of the people are sufficient to buy all the goods for sale, he simply repays his advance and keeps his profit. But on the other hand, if the total wages distributed by industry be not sufficient to buy all the products of industry, the retailer cannot repay all his debt unless the Credit Authority, through the (publicly-owned) Reserve Bank, issues consumer credit to bridge the gap. All the goods would then be sold, the consumer credit being cancelled when the retailer repays his advance. Thus would be preserved the stability of the measure of value, the just shekel on the one hand, and the just ephah on the other hand (with no destructive inflation of prices and the subsequent inevitable increased wage-claims).

The whole and sole purpose of any economic system should be to supply the needs of every creature. If the harvest is bountiful, or the ingenuity and labour of men have produced large numbers of desirable and useful manufactured articles, and if there is not enough money to buy it all, the amount of money should be correspondingly increased. The measure should not be lifeless gold in a vault, but the very goods themselves.

Thus we see the Divine Wisdom of the ancient Law of the perfect and just measure of value. Divine principles are NEVER out of date (Mark 12:30-31). Truth and justice are the same in all ages. Conditions may vary from age to age, but if righteous principles are the guide, it is always possible to devise a mechanism to suit the new conditions.

## 5. JESUS, ECONOMIST

When Jesus visited the Temple in Jerusalem, He made a scourge of cords and, overturning their tables, drove out the money changers, saying, "It is written, My House is the house of prayer: but ye have made it a den of thieves."

The law provided that, instead of driving the sacrificial lamb or kid all the way to Jerusalem, the pilgrim might sell it for money, and purchase another animal at Jerusalem (for the same price). There was nothing intrinsically wrong with the practice of selling beasts at the Temple. The sin of the dealers was the thievery of their exchange transactions (and inflated prices). It was another case of worldliness in the Church. Unrighteous economics earned His stern displeasure.

Jesus scathingly exposed another humbug. "God commanded, saying, Honour thy father and thy mother: and he that curseth father or mother, let him die the death. But ye say, Whosoever shall say to his father or his mother, it is a gift, by whatsoever thou mightest be profited by me; and honour not his father or mother, he shall be free. Thus ye have made the Commandment of God of none effect by your tradition (the Talmud). Ye hypocrites! . . ."

Jesus always upheld the authority of God's Commandments as expressed in the Books of Moses - The Torah. In the 5th, 6th, and 7th chapters of Matthew, commonly called the Sermon on the Mount, He taught the Gospel of the Kingdom of God. Referring to The Law, He said (Matt. 5:19-20,) "Whosoever shall break one of these least Commandments, and shall teach men so, he shall be called the least in the kingdom of heaven: but whosoever shall do and teach them, the same shall be called great in the kingdom of heaven. For I say unto you, That except your righteousness shall exceed the righteousness of the scribes (lawyers) and Pharisees (politicians), ye shall in NO case enter into the kingdom of heaven."

The Laws of Moses were thus confirmed by Jesus as The Laws of the Kingdom of God. The Economic Laws were included, for in 5:42 He expressly mentioned The Law of Lending. "Give to him that asketh thee, and from him that would borrow of thee turn not thou away." In Deuteronomy 15 quoted in Study 3, you will find the parallel in verses 7-10. "But thou shalt open thine hand wide unto him, and thou shalt surely lend him sufficient for his need." In Luke 6:34-35, Jesus said, "And if ye lend to them of whom ye hope to receive, what thank have ye? for sinners also lend to sinners to receive as much again. But love your enemies, and do good, and lend, hoping for nothing again; and your reward shall be great, and ye shall be the children of the Highest: for He is kind unto the unthankful and the evil."

In view of this confirmation of The Laws of Lending in the Books of Moses, what shall we say of those who uphold interest and security for loans? "<u>Hypocrites</u>" is the word applied to those who follow the traditions of men rather than The Law of God. What shall we say of the orthodox economist, professors of economics, those who determine bank policy, and their political henchmen, or even the Churches with their complicity with the debt and usury system of finance? (Matt. 23:13.) "Woe unto you, scribes (lawyers) and Pharisees (politicians), hypocrites! For ye shut up the kingdom of heaven against men: for ye neither go in yourselves, neither suffer ye them that are entering to go in."

"Ye cannot serve God and mammon." Many are eager to enjoy the New Era, the Kingdom of God on Earth, but the universal worship, by those in power, of the evil debt and interest system of mammon (that impoverishes and enslaves the masses) is the very thing which postpones God's Kingdom to the distant future (<u>now not so distant</u> - 2000).

During the slump I addressed the men in an unemployment camp on this subject. One of the audience objected that Jesus was an impractical oriental dreamer. The following words were the cause of his remark. (Matt. 6.) "Take no thought, saying, What shall we eat? or What shall we drink? or Wherewithal shall we be clothed? (For after all these things do the Gentiles seek:) for your heavenly Father knoweth that ye have need of all these things. But seek ye first the Kingdom (and Kingship) of God, and His righteousness; and all these things shall be added unto you."

Far from being the words of an impractical dreamer, this is the most profound economic declaration of all time. (Let us first pause to note that "Take no thought" would have been translated "Be not anxious.") Consider the practice of (privately-owned) trading banks issuing credit. The practice began when merchants were accustomed to lodge their gold and silver in the vaults of the goldsmiths. The gold certificates issued as receipts became accepted as current money in the place of gold. The goldsmiths soon discovered that they could issue and lend certificates greatly in excess of the gold which they held. They issued the paper out of nothing except the creditworthiness of the borrower, charged interest, and demanded gold, goods, or estate in repayment. Is that righteous? No! Yet the creation of credit by trading banks is exactly the same process. By following this unrighteous practice the world has become burdened with debt (to the people who own the banks - the "Hidden Hand" - the Synagogue of Satan - Rev. 2:9 & 3:9). "All these things," food, clothing, etc., instead of being added to us have been taken from us. If there is money to buy there is scarcity of goods, or when there is plenty, the money is lacking.

Why not seek the righteousness of God for a change? What is that righteousness? We have seen that God's Law assured economic freedom and security to ALL. Every family had its share of land. We have seen that in God's Law human need must be freely and gladly supplied, without usury, and without perpetual debt. God's Law enjoins lending for consumption, protects the consumer, and promises prosperity to the forgiving creditor. God's Law obeyed would provide ample for ALL, freedom from debt and crushing taxation. Therefore "Seek ye first the Kingdom of God, and His righteousness, and all these things shall be added unto you."

It is sometimes objected that the Social Credit idea of issuing credit and distributing it as pensions and national dividends would encourage laziness — "money for nothing." But it is not money for nothing. It is credit issued to represent something that has already been produced in excess of available purchasing power. Whereas it is evil for a trading bank to issue credit out of what the bank does not possess, it is right and proper for the people through their Government to issue credit to distribute that which they (or God) have already produced. Should the people forget that their standard of living depends upon their work and righteousness, and should they be tempted to sit back and enjoy the national dividend without pulling their weight, a rude awakening would be in store. With decreasing effort, the production would fall, and the national dividend would disappear.

But we have seen that new era, or the Kingdom of God, must be a Christian order and that Christ's standards must prevail. Worldly standards, the lust of the flesh, the desire of the eyes, and the pride of life, lead only to self-seeking, greed, oppression, poverty, crime, discord and conflict. Jesus set a new standard. "Whosoever will be great among you, let him be your minister; and whosoever will be chief among you, let him be your servant: even as the Son of Man came not to be ministered unto, but to minister, and to give his life a ransom for many."

Imbued with the spirit of service, every citizen will be eager to give the best to the common weal. There will be no more friction between sectional interests. In obedience to Divine Law, there will be economic freedom and security (instead of poverty and crime), there will be no longer the spur of fear to grab and hoard. There will be no longer competition to gain selfish advantage, but rather there will be competition to render service, and added joy and pride of the skilful craftsman, or husbandman. "And whatsoever ye do, do it heartily, as to the Lord, and not unto me. . . ." (Col. 3:23.). Amen.

www.ingramcontent.com/pod-product-compliance
Lightning Source LLC
Chambersburg PA
CBHW021433070526
44577CB00001B/181